UnlockU

7 Principles for Purpose Driven Growth

Tynetta Dance

©Copyright 2025 Tynetta Dance

All rights reserved. This book is protected under the copyright laws of the United States of America.

ISBN-13: 979-8-9929778-0-6

Library of Congress Control Number: 2025908020

No portion of this book may be reproduced, distributed, or transmitted in any form, including photocopying, recording, or other electronic or mechanical methods, without the written permission of the publisher, except in the case of brief quotations embodied in reviews and certain other non-commercial uses permitted by copyright law. Permission granted on request.

Dedication

To my children—Adrian, Taylor, and Logan:

I am so incredibly proud of each of you, and my love for you knows no bounds. You are my heart, my joy, and my reason for pushing forward every day. Know this: I am your #1 supporter and cheerleader. No matter where life takes you, no matter how big or small the challenges may seem, I will always stand beside you, lifting you up.

Learn from my mistakes and know that, as you grow, you'll be faced with choices that will test your character, your strength, and your heart. Now that you know better, you can do better. Don't be afraid to take risks. You only get one life to live, so make it one that is true to who you are and what you value and believe in.

Don't ever let anyone or anything stand in the way of your greatness. You are all capable of doing extraordinary things, and I am here to remind you of that each and every day. Walk in your purpose, unapologetically. Do not let fear or doubt stop you. You were born to stand tall, to shine brightly, and to create change in this world.

I love you all more than words can say. You are my everything.

With love, pride, and unwavering support,
Mom

Table of Contents

Preface vii

Introduction 1

CHAPTER 1:
Understand Who You Are and What You Want! 5

CHAPTER 2:
Never Compromise Your Morals or Values 15

CHAPTER 3:
Leverage Your Network and Exhaust All Resources 25

CHAPTER 4:
Operate Within Your Boundaries 37

CHAPTER 5:
Collaborate, Don't Compete 45

CHAPTER 6:
Know Your Worth 55

CHAPTER 7:
Unlock Your Growth Mindset and Uncover a
World of Endless Possibilities 65

CHAPTER 8:
Conclusion 75

Preface

To My Younger Self,

This book is for you, the young woman standing at the crossroads of uncertainty, dreams, and the first major steps into adulthood. There were moments of doubt, moments when you questioned your worth and your path, but if only you could see what I see now. You are stronger, more capable, and more resilient than you realize.

Trust your instincts. The whispers of your heart and the guidance of your inner voice will lead you to places you can't yet imagine. When the road feels uncertain or when others doubt you, trust that your intuition is a powerful compass. You've always known, deep down, what's best for you. Don't second-guess it.

Never give up on yourself. There will be times when the weight of challenges feels unbearable and the dream may seem just out of reach. But I promise you, perseverance will be your greatest ally. You are more than capable of turning every obstacle into an opportunity and every setback into a lesson. Keep going, even when it feels hard.

Don't lose focus on what you love and what truly matters to you. Life will throw many new roles your way: motherhood, career, relationships, and everything in between. But never lose sight of your dreams. They are not just fleeting wishes; they are the fuel that will keep you going when life gets busy and complicated. With every new experience, your dreams will evolve, but they will always be yours. Protect them fiercely and never let anyone dim your light.

Don't let anyone make you feel less than or like you don't belong. You were created with purpose and power. You belong in every room, at every table. Never shrink to make others comfortable. Walk in with confidence, knowing that you have every right to take up space.

Don't forget who you are and the bigger plan that God has in store for you. You were created with immense potential, and your life is part of a much larger story. Trust in the divine timing, and know that every step you take is leading you toward the greatness you were born to achieve.

The sky is the limit; you have everything you need to soar. Your future is waiting for you, and it's bigger, brighter, and more beautiful than you could ever imagine. All of your gifts, talents, and experiences have equipped you for this moment. You are ready.

And **don't allow yourself to succumb to your roles:** wife, mom, daughter, sister, friend, etc. You are all of those things, but they are not the totality of who you are. It's so easy to lose yourself in the demands of others, but it is critical to stay the course and remember to take care of yourself. You can't pour from an empty cup. You have to take the time to fill your own cup— mentally, physically, spiritually, and emotionally—so you can give your best and make a positive impact on the world around you.

Always walk in your purpose and never compromise your values. Your purpose is your guiding star. It will bring you fulfillment, peace, and alignment. And your values? They are the foundation that will anchor you through every storm. You'll never be perfect, so give yourself space and grace to be a perfectly flawed human. Don't be too hard on yourself. You are enough. You always have been and always will be.

Introduction

What if the key to achieving your dreams and unlocking your full potential was simply a matter of shifting your mindset and setting intentional goals? In this book, we'll explore the essential principles that can guide you on your journey of personal and professional growth, helping you understand who you truly are, what you want, and how to achieve it.

This book is a roadmap for anyone looking to break free of limiting beliefs and to unlock a world of possibilities through growth, self-reflection, and aligned action. The seven foundational principles outlined here are designed to help you transform your life, one empowered step at a time. By embracing these principles, you'll gain the tools, mindset, and strategies necessary to navigate life's challenges and achieve both your personal and professional goals.

Each principle works with all the others to create a comprehensive approach to personal growth, offering insights that will inspire you to take meaningful action and embrace the opportunities around you. Whether you're looking to achieve professional success, find deeper fulfillment, or overcome obstacles holding you back, these principles will guide you toward living a life that aligns with your highest potential.

Here's a brief overview of each principle you'll explore:

1. Understand Who You Are and What You Want
True growth begins with self-awareness. Understanding who you are—your values, strengths, and passions—provides clarity on what you truly want out of life. By gaining insight into your authentic self, you can set meaningful goals and create a path that aligns with your deepest desires. This principle teaches you the importance of self-reflection and how to identify your purpose so you can live a life of intention.

2. Never Compromise Your Morals or Values
Integrity is the foundation of lasting success. Life will often present situations where you are tempted to compromise your morals or values. But staying true to yourself ensures that you can live with confidence and peace of mind. In this principle, you'll learn how to make decisions that honor your core beliefs, and why protecting your values is key to achieving long-term fulfillment and success.

3. Leverage Your Network and Exhaust All Resources
No one achieves success in isolation. A strong network of mentors, peers, and advocates is crucial for growth. This principle emphasizes the power of building meaningful relationships and leveraging resources, whether it's knowledge,

tools, or opportunities, to support your journey. You'll learn how to nurture and tap into your network to open doors and accelerate your progress.

4. Operate Within Your Boundaries

Personal boundaries are essential to maintaining balance and well-being. Knowing your limits and creating healthy boundaries allows you to protect your energy, prioritize your goals, and avoid burnout. This principle teaches you how to set clear boundaries in all areas of life, ensuring that you honor both your needs and your ambitions without compromising your peace of mind.

5. Collaborate, Don't Compete

Collaboration leads to greater success than competition. This principle shifts the focus from rivalry to cooperation, teaching you how to leverage collective strength and create opportunities through collaboration. By working with others, you access diverse perspectives, skills, and resources that can propel you forward. You'll learn to embrace teamwork, building mutually beneficial relationships that foster long-term growth.

6. Know Your Worth

Self-worth is the key to confidence and success. When you know your value, you have the power to advocate for yourself, negotiate effectively, and make choices that reflect your worth. This principle guides you in recognizing your strengths, building confidence, and communicating your value in both personal and professional settings. By understanding your worth, you empower yourself to create opportunities and take bold steps toward reaching your goals.

7. Unlock Your Growth Mindset and Uncover a World of Endless Possibilities
A growth mindset is the belief that abilities and intelligence can be developed through effort and learning. This principle challenges you to view obstacles as opportunities for growth, embrace failure as feedback, and remain open to continuous improvement. By cultivating a growth mindset, you unlock endless possibilities for success and personal development, allowing you to achieve things you once thought were impossible.

Conclusion
These seven principles form the foundation for purpose-driven personal and professional growth. As you move through this book, you'll be equipped with the strategies, mindset, and tools to navigate challenges, make confident decisions, and achieve your fullest potential. Let's dive in and begin unlocking the life you were meant to live!

CHAPTER 1

Understand Who You Are and What You Want!

The first step in any meaningful transformation is understanding who you are and what you truly want. This is the foundation of personal growth. Without clarity about your values, strengths, and desires, it's nearly impossible to create a life of purpose and fulfillment. Self-awareness allows you to make better decisions, align your actions with your goals, and move forward with confidence.

The Importance of Self-Awareness and Clarity in Life

Self-awareness is the cornerstone of growth. When you know yourself, your core values, your strengths, your passions, and even your weaknesses, you gain clarity about what you want from life. This understanding doesn't just help you make more informed decisions; it guides you toward the goals that truly matter to you, not those imposed by external pressures.

Self-reflection is the key to unlocking this clarity. The more time you dedicate to understanding your own motivations, desires, and values, the more you'll uncover about what drives you. Once you know who you are, it's easier to chart a course toward the life you want.

Techniques for Self-Reflection: Journaling, Meditation, and Personality Assessments

There are various ways to reflect on your life and values. Choose the techniques that resonate with you, but here are a few tools to help you get started:

- **Journaling**: Writing is an excellent way to tap into your thoughts and emotions. Take a few minutes each day to journal about what's going on in your life, how you're feeling, and what you hope to achieve. Over time, you'll notice patterns in your thoughts that reveal your true desires and values.

- **Meditation**: Meditation can help quiet your mind and connect you with your inner self. Even a few minutes of mindfulness each day can help you focus on what matters most to you and clear out distractions.

- **Personality Assessments**: Tools like the Myers-Briggs Type Indicator (MBTI), the StrengthsFinder assessment, DISC, or the Enneagram can give you deeper insight into your natural preferences, strengths, and opportunities for growth. These tools help you understand how you interact with the world, making it easier to align your decisions with your strengths.

Identifying Core Values, Strengths, and Passions

To truly understand who you are, you must dig deeper into the following areas:

- **Core Values**: Your values are the principles that guide your decisions and actions. They are the things you hold dear, such as honesty, family, integrity, creativity, or freedom. Identifying your core values is crucial for building a life that aligns with your true self.

- **Strengths**: What are you naturally good at? Recognizing your strengths allows you to leverage them to reach your goals. Focus on what comes easily to you and where you excel. This might include skills like communication, problem-solving, and/or leadership.

- **Passions**: What lights you up? Your passions are the things that fuel your energy and enthusiasm. Whether it's art, helping others, or solving complex problems, your passions provide insight into what you want to spend your time and energy on.

Once you identify your core values, strengths, and passions, you'll begin to see the blueprint for the life you want to create.

Creating Your Personal Purpose Statement

One of the most powerful ways to bring clarity to your life is by crafting a **Personal Purpose Statement.** This statement helps you align your values, interests, and strengths into a singular focus, giving you a clear direction for the choices you make and the goals you set.

Your purpose statement is a reflection of your true self—a guiding principle that will keep you grounded as you move forward. It encapsulates who you are, why you're here, and how you plan to serve the world. Here's a simple structure for crafting yours:

My purpose is to (*insert desire/interest*) **because I** (*insert core value*). **I will do this by** (*insert strength*).

For example:
"**My purpose is to** *inspire and empower others to live with confidence and clarity because I deeply value personal growth and the power of transformation. I*

will do this by using my strengths in leadership and emotional intelligence to guide and support others in unlocking their full potential."

This statement connects your core value (personal growth and transformation), your passion (empowering others), and your strengths (leadership and emotional intelligence). It gives you a roadmap for how you will contribute to the world, and it can help you navigate the decisions and actions that follow.

Setting Meaningful and Authentic Goals

Once you have a clearer understanding of your values, strengths, and passions, it's time to set goals that truly reflect your authentic self. Goal-setting isn't about following someone else's dream for you, it's about creating goals that align with who you are and what you want.

SMART Goals: One of the most effective methods for setting clear and actionable goals is the SMART framework. SMART stands for ***Specific, Measurable, Achievable, Relevant, and Time-bound.*** This method ensures your goals are realistic and actionable, helping you stay focused on what truly matters.

Example:

- **Specific**: I will improve my work-life balance by dedicating at least two hours each evening to personal time.

- **Measurable**: I will track my progress by journaling about how I spend my evenings each week.

- **Achievable**: I will prioritize my schedule to make room for my personal time.

- **Relevant**: This goal supports my core value of family and self-care.

- **Time-bound**: I will implement this change for the next month and review my progress.

This SMART goal reflects the importance of self-care (a core value) and helps you take actionable steps toward a more balanced life.

Aligning Your Actions with Your Values and Goals

Once you've set meaningful, authentic goals, it's time to ensure your actions align with them. This requires consistent reflection and self-evaluation. Regularly assess whether your day-to-day choices are moving you closer to your desired outcomes or pushing you farther from them.

For example, if your core value is family, but you're spending all your time at work, you may need to reconsider how you allocate your time. If one of your passions is fitness, but you're not prioritizing exercise, you may need to make it a non-negotiable part of your routine.

The Importance of Regular Reflection and Reassessment

Self-awareness is not a one-time exercise. It's a lifelong process that requires regular reflection and reassessment. As you grow and evolve, so will your values and goals. Make it a habit to revisit your goals and values periodically, adjusting them as needed to stay true to who you are and what you want.

Example: Clarifying Your Values, Strengths, and Goals

Let's walk through an example of how you can apply these concepts. Imagine you've identified the following:

- **Core Values**: Family, Integrity, Personal Growth

- **Strengths**: Emotional Intelligence, Leadership, Creativity

- **Passions**: Helping others, Traveling, Writing

Based on these, you could set a goal like:

"I will create a blog to share personal growth strategies and travel tips, aiming to inspire and help others achieve balance in their lives."

This goal aligns with your values (*helping others, personal growth*), leverages your strengths (*creativity, leadership*), and feeds your passions (*writing, traveling*). By creating specific, measurable, attainable, relevant, and time-bound steps, you can make this goal a reality.

Conclusion

Understanding who you are and what you want is the cornerstone of personal growth. By clarifying your values, strengths, and passions, you gain the self-awareness needed to set authentic goals and make decisions that align with your true self. Once you have this clarity, you can begin to create a life that reflects your most authentic desires, one that is purposeful, fulfilling, and aligned with your highest potential.

Reflection:

"Clarity begins within; when you understand who you are and what you truly want, every step forward becomes a path toward your purpose."

As you embark on this journey of personal growth, it's essential to start with a deep understanding of who you are and what you truly want. This foundational knowledge will serve as your compass, guiding your decisions, actions, and the goals you set along the way. In Chapter 1, we explored how self-awareness and clarity can unlock your potential, helping you align your life with your authentic self. I challenge you to take a moment to explore your identity and desires to set the stage for your transformative experience.

1. What are your top three core values, and how do they shape your decisions?
2. Identify your greatest strengths and explain how they can help you reach your goals.
3. Which activities ignite your passion, and why are they important to you?
4. How can you align your actions with your values and strengths to create a fulfilling life?
5. Write a personal purpose statement that combines your values, strengths, and passions: "My purpose is to [*desire*] because I [*core value*]. I will achieve this by [*strength*]."

Notes

CHAPTER 2

Never Compromise Your Morals or Values

The Importance of Integrity

In Chapter 1, we focused on the importance of self-awareness, understanding your values, strengths, and passions, and how they guide your decisions and actions. Now that you have a clearer understanding of who you are, it's time to take a deeper look at your morals and values and learn how to protect them. Integrity isn't just about doing what's right in the big moments, it's about staying true to your core beliefs in every decision you make, big or small.

Integrity is the ability to look yourself in the mirror each day and know you did the right thing for the right reasons, even when it's difficult, inconvenient, or unpopular. This concept goes beyond following the rules. It's about aligning your actions with your values, even when no one is watching, and choosing what's right over what's easy.

Your values are the moral compass that guides you through life. They shape how you interact with the world, how you approach challenges, and how you treat others. When we compromise on these values, it can cause internal conflict and lead to a sense of disconnection from our true selves. In this chapter, we'll dive into how staying true to your morals not only builds integrity but also leads to long-term success, self-respect, and personal fulfillment.

Defining Personal Ethics and Values

Your **values** are the principles that guide your decisions and behaviors. They are deeply personal and reflect what matters most to you, whether it's honesty, respect, family, creativity, or justice. When you live by your values, you feel more aligned with your true self, which is essential for long-term fulfillment.

On the other hand, personal ethics are the set of moral standards that inform how you act in the world. Your ethics are often informed by your values, but they can also be shaped by the culture, environment, and experiences that you've had.

The Impact of Compromising Your Morals

Compromising on your morals or values may seem like a small concession at first, but it can have profound effects over time. Each time you compromise, you begin to erode your sense of self-respect and personal integrity. Over time, this can lead to a feeling of disconnection from who you really are.

Example of Compromising Values: The Business Leader

Let's say a business leader is offered a high-paying contract with a company that engages in practices that do not align with their environmental values. This leader might feel tempted to take the deal, reasoning that the financial rewards are substantial and could offer growth opportunities. However, taking this deal would require ignoring the leader's commitment to environmental sustainability, a core value.

Despite the pressure, the leader decides to reject the deal. While initially disappointing, the leader's decision to stay true to their values leads to long-term respect within their industry and a deeper sense of fulfillment. They realize that success built on integrity is far more valuable than any short-term financial gain. More importantly, they can look in the mirror each day knowing they made the right choice for the right reasons.

How to Align Your Decisions with Your Morals

Just as we learned in the previous chapter how to clarify our **values** and set SMART goals, in this chapter, we'll take it a step further by exploring how to align your actions with your core principles. This is key to ensuring that you make decisions that honor your values every time.

Example of a Purpose Statement

Remember the purpose statement from Chapter 1:

> *"My purpose is to inspire and empower others to live with confidence and clarity because I deeply value personal growth and the power of transformation. I will do this by using my strengths in leadership and emotional intelligence to guide and support others in unlocking their full potential."*

This statement reflects both their values (personal growth) and strengths (leadership and emotional intelligence), which they can use as a framework for making aligned decisions.

When faced with difficult situations, this purpose statement can be used as a compass to guide decisions. If the same business leader from the earlier example had a purpose statement like, *"My purpose is to promote sustainable business practices because I value environmental stewardship,"* this would make rejecting the unethical contract an easier decision. The purpose statement helps to keep them aligned with their core values.

Being able to look yourself in the mirror means making decisions that you can stand behind—no matter how hard or unpopular those decisions may be.

The Power of Integrity: Looking Yourself in the Mirror

The real test of integrity is how you feel about yourself when no one is looking. It's about knowing that you've done the right thing, even when it was difficult or when it cost you something. When you act with integrity, you live with the peace of mind that comes from knowing your decisions are rooted in your authentic values.

When you know you've made the right decision, even if others don't understand or agree, you create a sense of inner peace. That's the essence of integrity: being able to stand by your choices, regardless of external approval, because you've acted in line with your beliefs.

Example: *The Honest Student and Academic Integrity*

Imagine a student faced with the decision to cheat on an exam. Their classmates are doing it, and it feels like the easiest way to get ahead. However, they know that honesty and integrity are core values for them. Despite the pressure, they decide to study honestly and trust that doing so will lead to long-term success, even if it's harder in the short term.

That student walks out of the exam knowing they made the right decision, even if it wasn't the most popular one. They can look themselves in the mirror with pride, knowing they upheld their values, regardless of the outcome. This peace of mind is the reward for acting with integrity.

The Benefits of Staying True to Your Values

While staying true to your values may not always be easy, the rewards are profound. Here's what happens when you align your decisions with your morals:

- **Authenticity**: You live in alignment with your true self, which brings peace of mind and fulfillment. There's no internal conflict when your actions match your values.

- **Respect**: Others begin to respect and trust you because they know you'll make decisions based on your integrity, not on convenience or external pressures.

- **Long-Term Success**: Success achieved through alignment with your values is far more sustainable. When you honor your principles, you create a legacy that others admire and trust.

- **Peace of Mind**: Integrity leads to peace of mind. You know that every decision you make is rooted in your most authentic self. The ultimate reward is the ability to look in the mirror and feel proud of who you are and what you stand for.

Example: The Leader Who Refused to Cut Corners

Let's return to our business leader from earlier. When they chose to turn down a lucrative but unethical contract, they could have taken the easier path. However, their decision was guided by their value of environmental sustainability. In the long run, their decision didn't just preserve their integrity, it solidified their reputation as a leader who values ethics over profits. This made them more respected in their industry, earned them trust from clients, and led to long-term, sustainable success.

By staying true to their core values, they could look in the mirror every day, knowing they made decisions for the right reasons, even when it was difficult.

Conclusion

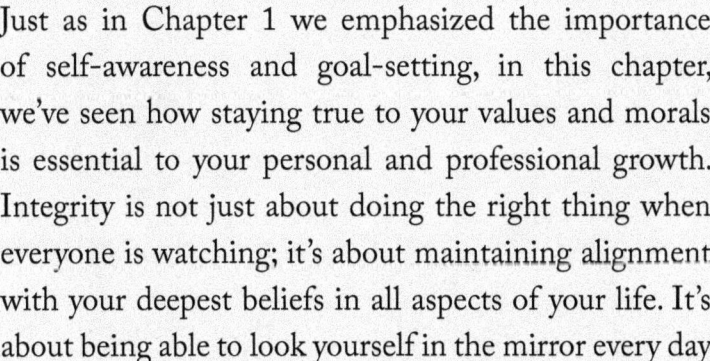

Just as in Chapter 1 we emphasized the importance of self-awareness and goal-setting, in this chapter, we've seen how staying true to your values and morals is essential to your personal and professional growth. Integrity is not just about doing the right thing when everyone is watching; it's about maintaining alignment with your deepest beliefs in all aspects of your life. It's about being able to look yourself in the mirror every day and know you acted with integrity, even when it was difficult or unpopular.

By protecting your integrity and consistently making decisions that reflect your values, you build a strong foundation for lasting success, meaningful relationships, and a life that truly reflects your authentic self. When you choose not to compromise your morals, you unlock a life of greater fulfillment, peace, and trust.

Reflection:

"Don't trade your authenticity for approval." ~*Unknown*

Now that you've explored the core elements of self-awareness and goal-setting, it's time to reflect on how you can apply these insights to your personal journey. Use the following questions to build on your thoughts from Chapter 1:

1. How do your core values guide the prioritization of your long-term goals?
2. What strategies ensure your daily actions align with your long-term vision?
3. How can regular reflection help you adapt your goals to evolving values?
4. What challenges might arise in staying true to your personal purpose, and how can you overcome them?
5. How can external feedback and self-reflection together help you measure and stay on track with your goals?

Notes

CHAPTER 3

Leverage Your Network and Exhaust All Resources

In Chapters 1 and 2, we explored the importance of self-awareness and integrity, building a solid foundation of who you are, and aligning your actions with your core values. This self-awareness is crucial for setting meaningful goals and making informed decisions. But even the most self-aware individuals need resources, people, knowledge, and opportunities that can support and propel them forward.

No one achieves success in isolation. To truly scale your growth, you need more than just clarity about your values; you need to tap into the network and resources around you. In this chapter, we'll explore how to build and leverage your network, utilize your education and experience, and tap into the right tools to maximize your potential. We'll also discuss the vital roles of coaching, mentoring, and other relationships within your network, and why it's important to have the right people and support at your table.

The Power of a Strong and Supportive Network

While self-awareness and integrity form the foundation for success, the relationships you cultivate are the pillars that sustain and elevate your growth. A strong and diverse network of mentors, coaches, peers, advocates, and sponsors is one of the most valuable resources you can build.

Your network is not just about accumulating contacts, it's about nurturing meaningful, mutually supportive relationships that align with your values and goals. These relationships offer crucial insights, guidance, accountability, and, importantly, opportunities that you might not find on your own. Having the right people in your corner is one of the most powerful ways to accelerate your progress.

But how do you leverage these relationships effectively? The key is understanding the distinct roles each person in your network can play and aligning your needs with their strengths.

Coaching and Mentoring: Understanding the Roles

To leverage your network effectively, it's important to distinguish between two key forms of support: coaching and mentoring. Both are integral to your growth but serve distinct purposes.

- **Coaching** is a collaborative relationship where the coach's role is to help you unlock your potential. Through powerful questions, frameworks, and reflective exercises, coaches help you discover solutions for yourself, develop actionable steps, and push you toward your goals. Coaching is future-oriented and performance-driven, helping you to stay accountable and improve your skills.

- **Mentoring,** on the other hand, is a guidance-based relationship where the mentor shares wisdom and strategic insights based on their own experience. Mentors help you navigate long-term challenges and offer advice for big decisions, drawing from their experience to offer you direction and perspective. Mentorship tends to be more reflective and focused on broadening your view of your path, not necessarily on tactical actions.

Both coaching and mentoring complement each other perfectly. Mentors provide the strategic direction, while coaches offer tools and frameworks to help you execute that vision.

Example: The Career Professional Seeking Both Mentorship and Coaching

Consider a professional looking to move into a leadership role. She needs both strategic advice and actionable steps to succeed.

- She reaches out to a mentor with extensive leadership experience. The mentor offers guidance on navigating corporate culture, managing teams, and making high-level decisions. The mentor helps her develop a long-term vision for her career, showing her where she might be able to grow and offering insight into leadership challenges she might face.

- At the same time, she works with a coach who specializes in leadership development. The coach doesn't offer advice but instead helps her explore her own leadership style, strengths, and areas for growth. Through structured conversations, the coach helps her build the confidence to speak up in meetings, improve communication skills, and develop strategies that feel authentic to her.

By combining mentorship and coaching, she gains both the wisdom of experience and a clear, actionable plan to take steps toward her leadership goals.

Building Your Circle: Coaches, Mentors, Advocates, Sponsors, and Peers

To maximize the effectiveness of your network, it's important to understand the different roles that people can play in your growth. Beyond coaches and mentors, your network should also include advocates, sponsors, and peers, each of whom plays a distinct role.

1. **Coaches**: Coaches are there to help you unlock your potential through powerful questioning and guidance. They don't provide the answers but help you find them. A coach's job is to help you move from where you are to where you want to be by challenging you and helping you take consistent action.

2. **Mentors**: Mentors share their experience, offering advice and strategic direction. They help you navigate your career path, share their wisdom, and help you learn from their successes and mistakes.

3. **Advocates**: Advocates actively champion your cause. They speak highly of you behind closed doors, recommend you for opportunities, and help elevate your visibility. Advocates often have influence in your industry or organization and can help open doors for you.

4. **Sponsors**: Sponsors go one step further than advocates; they actively invest in your career. They

recommend you for promotions, advocate for your success within their networks, and put their own reputation on the line to help advance your career.

5. **Peers**: Peers are an essential part of your support system, even though they may not have the same level of experience or influence as mentors or sponsors. Peers provide mutual support, encouragement, and feedback. They offer a shared experience that can help you navigate challenges together.

Each of these roles is necessary and plays a unique part in your growth and success. You don't have to navigate your journey alone—build a circle that provides a full spectrum of support and leverage each person's strengths.

Exhausting All Resources: Tools, Knowledge, and Opportunities

Beyond your network, there are other vital resources you can tap into to fuel your growth. These include formal education, prior experience, and external resources such as books, workshops, and networking opportunities.

1. **Formal Education**: Your educational background provides you with foundational knowledge and credibility. But growth doesn't stop once you leave school. Continual learning through workshops, courses, and/

or certifications can keep you **current** in your field and expand your expertise.

2. **Prior Experience**: Reflect on the challenges and achievements from your past roles. Your experiences have shaped your leadership abilities, problem-solving skills, and decision-making processes. Don't underestimate the lessons you've already learned.

3. **Books, Podcasts, and Industry Resources**: These external resources help you stay informed and provide fresh insights into your field. Diverse sources of information allow you to view challenges from new perspectives and approach problems creatively.

4. **Opportunities**: Seek out opportunities, whether through networking, projects, or side ventures, that can help you gain new skills, grow your influence, or accelerate your career path. Every opportunity is a chance to expand your horizons.

Example: The Entrepreneur Who Leverages All Resources

Consider an entrepreneur looking to scale their business. They're working with a mentor for strategic advice and a coach to refine their leadership skills, but they're also tapping into other resources:

- Read books on marketing and growth strategies.
- Attend networking events to build relationships with potential investors.
- Leverage their formal education in business to guide their decision-making.
- Participate in online courses to improve their sales and marketing techniques.

By exhausting all available resources, the entrepreneur maximizes their opportunities for growth and business development.

Conclusion

In this chapter, we've delved into the power of a strong and supportive network, highlighting the critical roles that mentors, coaches, advocates, sponsors, and peers play in your growth. We've also explored how to leverage your education, experience, and various resources to maximize your potential.

Success is not achieved in isolation. By building and nurturing meaningful relationships and utilizing the resources available to you, you create a dynamic support system that propels you forward. Whether it's through strategic guidance from mentors, actionable frameworks from coaches, or new opportunities discovered through networking, each element of your network contributes to your journey toward success.

Remember, leveraging your network and resources isn't just about asking for help; it's about creating a mutually beneficial ecosystem where both you and your network grow together. Reflect on the relationships you have and the resources you can tap into, and take deliberate steps to strengthen and expand them.

By thoughtfully engaging with your network and exhausting the resources at your disposal, you set the stage for continuous growth and success.

Reflection:

"Leveraging resources, building partnerships, and making strategic connections unlock opportunities and drive true growth."

As we conclude this chapter, take a moment to reflect on how you can apply these concepts to your own journey. Leveraging your network and resources is a crucial step in building on the self-awareness and integrity you've cultivated so far. Use the following questions to help deepen your understanding and create a clear plan for action.

1. How can your values, strengths, and passions guide the type of people to include in your network?
2. Which areas of your life or career could benefit most from mentorship or support, and who could fill these roles?
3. Who in your current network supports your growth, and what gaps do you need to address?
4. How can you contribute meaningfully to your network while also leveraging it for your growth?
5. What action can you take this week to strengthen a key relationship or explore new resources for development?

Notes

Notes

CHAPTER 4

Operate Within Your Boundaries

In the previous chapters, we've discussed the importance of self-awareness, integrity, and leveraging your network to propel your growth. We've explored how to build meaningful relationships and utilize resources to unlock your potential. But there's one more crucial element in your journey toward success: operating within your boundaries.

Without clear boundaries, even the most well-constructed plans and relationships can lead to burnout, frustration, and a sense of imbalance. Boundaries are essential for maintaining your focus, protecting your time, and ensuring that you stay aligned with your values. Just as we've emphasized the importance of self-awareness in Chapters 1 and 2, setting and honoring your boundaries is equally foundational for long-term success.

In this chapter, we'll explore how to set and uphold boundaries, both with yourself and others, and why doing so is vital for staying balanced and avoiding burnout. We'll also discuss the empowering role of *"no"* as a complete sentence, a simple but powerful tool for protecting your time and energy.

Understanding the Importance of Boundaries

Setting boundaries begins with understanding your personal limits. To protect your well-being and focus, you first need to have a clear understanding of what you need, whether it's time, space, or emotional energy. When you've spent time cultivating self-awareness, as we discussed earlier, you are in a much better position to identify the boundaries that will help you honor your values and purpose.

When your boundaries align with your goals, they allow you to prioritize the things that matter most, such as family, career growth, or personal development, while saying no to the distractions that drain your energy.

> *Example*: Consider the corporate professional who is balancing leadership development with everyday work responsibilities. She sets clear boundaries by allocating time each week to reflect on her goals and refine her leadership skills. By doing so, she ensures she can remain focused and engaged in her career development while also managing her day-to-day tasks.

Setting Boundaries for Yourself and Others

It's one thing to set boundaries; it's another to uphold them consistently. Boundaries aren't just for protecting your time, they also protect your focus, your energy, and your mental well-being. Setting clear boundaries means honoring them, both with yourself and with others.

When you don't enforce your boundaries, you run the risk of spreading yourself too thin and failing to follow through on what truly matters. Whether it's saying no to an unimportant meeting or communicating your need for personal time, upholding your boundaries ensures you can stay focused on the goals that align with your purpose statement.

It's also important to set boundaries with others, especially in work environments where demands on your time can be relentless. A lack of boundaries often leads to resentment—you begin to feel taken advantage of when you consistently put others' needs before your own. Effective communication is key here. Being direct and assertive about your limits ensures respect from others, while also safeguarding your own needs.

> *Example*: Let's revisit the aspiring executive who is looking to step into a senior leadership role. As she takes on additional responsibilities, she realizes that she's often sacrificing her personal time and well-being to meet expectations. She sets boundaries by clearly communicating her limits to her team and supervisors,

such as scheduling "office hours" for team collaboration and taking evenings off for personal time. This helps her focus on her long-term leadership development while preserving her mental health and focus.

The Power of "No" and Avoiding Burnout

The word *"no"* is a complete sentence. It is a simple yet powerful tool for maintaining boundaries. Saying no allows you to preserve your energy for the things that truly align with your values and goals. It can be difficult to say no, especially when others' needs feel urgent or important. But by saying no to what doesn't serve you, you free up space to say yes to what truly matters.

Burnout is often the result of saying yes to too many things, whether it's additional tasks, unnecessary meetings, or social obligations that drain your time and energy. When you fail to uphold your boundaries, you spread yourself too thin, and your ability to perform at your best diminishes. Saying no is essential for protecting your focus, your creativity, and your mental health.

> *Example*: The entrepreneur we discussed earlier has learned to manage her growing business while honoring her personal boundaries. She recognizes that answering client emails at all hours of the night isn't sustainable, so she starts saying no to work after her designated hours.

This helps her avoid burnout and maintain her enthusiasm for her business, ensuring that her work remains high quality and aligned with her values.

Consequences of Not Honoring Your Boundaries

Failing to honor your boundaries comes with several consequences. The most immediate is burnout, feeling physically exhausted, mentally overwhelmed, and emotionally drained. It is impossible to pour from an empty cup! Without boundaries, it becomes difficult to focus on what matters most, leading to a decrease in productivity, focus, and satisfaction.

When you fail to set or respect boundaries, resentment can also build up, toward colleagues, clients, friends, or even yourself. If you're constantly overcommitting and neglecting your own needs, you begin to feel taken advantage of. This can erode your relationships and undermine your own sense of worth.

Last, operating without boundaries can lead to distracted decision-making. When you don't have the time or energy to think critically, your ability to make informed, strategic decisions suffers. Boundaries create the mental space necessary to process information, reflect on your goals, and stay focused on your path forward.

Conclusion

Setting and upholding boundaries is a key practice in maintaining balance, focus, and well-being. By establishing clear limits around your time, energy, and priorities, you protect yourself from burnout and ensure that your actions align with your core values and purpose. Boundaries are not just about saying "no" to others, they're about saying "yes" to yourself, your goals, and your vision for the future.

The power of boundaries lies in their ability to help you stay on track, maintain balance, and protect your mental and emotional health. By consistently honoring your limits, you ensure that you have the energy and focus necessary to achieve sustainable success and growth.

Reflection:

"Boundaries aren't walls to keep people out, they're bridges that protect your peace and allow real connections."

To deepen your understanding and ensure that the insights from this chapter resonate with your personal journey, take time to reflect on the following questions. These prompts will help you consider how to effectively set and honor boundaries, building on the self-awareness, integrity, and network you've cultivated in the previous chapters.

1. What key areas in your life require stronger boundaries, and how do they align with your core values and goals?
2. Reflect on a recent situation where maintaining a boundary was challenging. What could you do differently next time?
3. How can you become more assertive in saying "no" to requests that don't align with your purpose?
4. How can setting clear boundaries help you prevent burnout and maintain balance?
5. How do your boundaries impact your relationships, and what steps can you take to ensure those boundaries are respected?

Notes

CHAPTER 5

Collaborate, Don't Compete

In the previous chapters, we've explored how self-awareness, integrity, and boundaries create the foundation for sustainable success. We've also discussed how to leverage your network and resources effectively to propel you forward. Now, let's dive into a crucial aspect of your growth: the power of collaboration.

In a world that often emphasizes competition, it's easy to fall into the trap of thinking that success is a zero-sum game, that someone else's win is your loss. But true success isn't about outshining others or proving yourself better. It's about collaborating with others to elevate everyone's potential and create a collective path to success.

This chapter explores the value of collaboration over competition, strategies for building strong, effective teams, and why shared knowledge and diverse perspectives can be the key to unlocking innovative solutions and growth.

The Power of Collaboration Over Competition

When you collaborate, you invite others into the process of growth and learning. Collaboration fosters an environment of mutual respect and shared success, where everyone benefits. On the other hand, competition often leads to individualistic thinking, where people focus on outperforming others instead of growing together.

Here's a powerful saying I once heard:

> *"Secure people collaborate, insecure people compete."*
> *~Unknown*

This statement captures an essential truth: Confidence in your own abilities and potential allows you to see the value in others, work with them, and build something greater than what you could achieve on your own. Insecurity, on the other hand, drives the need to prove yourself at the expense of others. It limits your vision and makes success feel like a battle to be fought alone.

When you embrace collaboration, you shift your focus from comparison to co-creation. You stop viewing others as threats and start seeing them as strategic partners in your shared journey. By collaborating with others, you expand your horizons, learn from different perspectives, and grow in ways that wouldn't be possible through competition alone.

Strategies for Fostering Teamwork and Collective Success

To truly leverage the power of collaboration, you need to cultivate an environment that encourages teamwork and collective success. Here are several strategies to help you foster effective collaboration:

1. **Embrace the Value of Diverse Perspectives**: When you collaborate with others, you invite new ideas, solutions, and experiences that you might not have considered. In every team, there are different skills, strengths, and worldviews. By embracing diversity, you create opportunities for innovation and creative problem-solving. A truly collaborative environment is one where all voices are heard, valued, and integrated.

   Example: Think back to that career professional who worked with both a mentor and a coach to enhance her leadership skills. When she collaborated with colleagues and team members, she was able to apply insights from her diverse support system, creating a stronger, more effective team dynamic. The collective success of the team became a direct reflection of the power of collaboration.

2. **Encourage Open Communication and Trust**: Trust is the foundation of any successful collaboration. Without it, team members hesitate to share ideas, ask

questions, or take risks. **Open communication** is key to building that trust. When you create an environment where people feel safe to express themselves, collaborate freely, and make mistakes without fear of judgment, you unlock the collective potential of the group.

3. **Focus on Collective Goals, Not Individual Recognition**: One of the most important aspects of collaboration is having a shared vision. Whether you're working on a project, a team, or a long-term goal, aligning everyone around a collective purpose ensures that everyone is working toward the same outcome. When the success of the team is more important than individual recognition, the entire group is motivated to contribute to each other's success.

The Benefits of Strategic Partnerships

One of the greatest advantages of collaboration is the opportunity to build strategic partnerships. Strategic partnerships involve working together with individuals or organizations that complement your strengths and abilities, creating an ecosystem where each party brings something valuable to the table.

- **Access to New Resources**: By partnering with others, you gain access to resources, knowledge, and opportunities that you may not have had on your own. These resources can include capital, expertise, networks, or technology, tools that help you scale your efforts and increase your chances of success.

- **Amplification of Impact**: When you collaborate strategically, you amplify your impact. Think of it like this: if you're a small business owner looking to grow, collaborating with another business can expand your reach, share costs, and create joint offerings that neither party could achieve alone.

- **Increased Learning Opportunities**: Strategic partnerships create the chance to learn from others, whether it's a mentor who can offer industry insights or a colleague who has complementary skills. This exchange of knowledge helps both parties grow in their own roles and understand different approaches to problem-solving.

Example: Think back to the entrepreneur who successfully scaled their business by leveraging diverse resources, including books, seminars, and networking events. They also forged strategic partnerships with other businesses, allowing them to increase their brand visibility and access new markets. This strategic collaboration allowed them to create a larger, more sustainable business than they could have achieved on their own.

Overcoming the Fear of Competition and Focusing on Collective Growth

Fear of competition can often paralyze us and prevent effective collaboration. The anxiety of not measuring up or the fear of losing out on opportunities can prevent us from working together with others. But this fear is often rooted in scarcity thinking, which assumes that there isn't enough success or opportunity to go around.

Instead, when you adopt an abundance mindset, you shift your focus from scarcity to the understanding that there is enough opportunity for everyone. By focusing on collective growth, you elevate not only your own success but the success of those around you.

To move past the fear of competition, it's important to remind yourself that collaboration isn't about giving up your power, it's about multiplying it. When you work with others, you harness the collective energy of the group to reach new heights.

Conclusion

Success is not a solo endeavor. While individual achievement is important, the true power lies in collaboration. When you embrace collaboration over competition, you unlock new possibilities for growth, creativity, and innovation. By focusing on shared goals, building strategic partnerships, and learning from diverse perspectives, you elevate not just yourself but everyone you work with.

Collaboration is a mindset, one that fosters teamwork, trust, and mutual respect. It's a mindset that allows you to see others not as rivals, but as partners in a larger mission. When you collaborate, you create a network of collective successes, one where everyone has the opportunity to thrive.

Reflection:

"Collaboration is the true catalyst for growth. In a world of abundance, we thrive by partnering and elevating each other."

As we continue our journey to understanding ourselves, setting boundaries, and leveraging our networks, it's time to shift our focus to the power of collaboration. Let's reflect on how integrating these foundational principles can enhance our ability to work with others toward shared success.

Reflection Questions:

1. How has your approach to collaboration versus competition affected outcomes, and what would you do differently next time?
2. How can embracing diverse perspectives within your network enhance your personal or professional growth?
3. What steps can you take to build trust and open communication in your collaborations, and how do these align with your boundaries and self-awareness?
4. Identify a potential strategic partnership. What strengths or resources could it bring, and how might it help you achieve your goals?
5. How can aligning around collective goals improve team or community success, and how does this relate to maintaining your personal boundaries?

Notes

Notes

CHAPTER 6

Know Your Worth

In the previous chapters, we've explored the importance of self-awareness, integrity, and collaboration, all essential components for building a strong foundation for growth. But there's one more crucial step that ties everything together: knowing your worth.

When you truly understand your value, both personally and professionally, you step into a place of empowerment. You stop questioning whether you deserve success or the opportunities that come your way. You learn to advocate for yourself and, most importantly, you stop letting self-limiting beliefs or imposter syndrome defeat you. This chapter is about understanding your worth, building confidence, overcoming fear, and asserting your place at the table.

The Importance of Self-Value in Personal and Professional Settings

Knowing your worth is not just an abstract concept. It's about recognizing the unique contributions you bring to every aspect of your life, whether that's in your relationships or your career. Understanding your worth empowers you to navigate the world from a place of strength and certainty.

- **Personal Worth**: On a personal level, knowing your worth means recognizing the core values and qualities that define who you are. It's understanding that your self-esteem doesn't come from external validation but from an internal belief in your abilities, values, and potential. When you honor your own worth, you establish healthy boundaries, avoid toxic relationships, and demand the respect you deserve.

- **Professional Worth**: In the professional world, understanding your worth means being aware of your skills, experience, and the impact you have. When you recognize your value in the workplace, you stop doubting whether you deserve promotions, raises, or new opportunities. Knowing your worth helps you navigate the professional world with confidence and ensures you're not overlooked or undervalued.

Recognizing and Advocating for Your Own Worth

One of the toughest battles many face is recognizing their own worth, especially when they are surrounded by people who don't seem to see it. We've all experienced moments where we feel like we don't belong, like we're not qualified enough or capable enough to claim our seat at the table. That's where imposter syndrome can creep in.

It's essential to acknowledge this feeling, but also to recognize that it doesn't define you. Imposter syndrome is simply a result of self-doubt—not a reflection of your true potential. You belong in every room you're in. You've earned your seat through your skills, your efforts, and your achievements. The key is recognizing your value and advocating for it.

> *Example*: Recall the career professional who had been diligently working with her mentor and coach. There were times when she struggled with self-doubt, wondering if she was ready to step into a senior leadership role. But by reflecting on her journey, the growth she had experienced, and the value she brought to her team, she was able to push past imposter syndrome. When an opportunity for promotion arose, she confidently advocated for herself, knowing she was not only ready but deserving of the position.

Practical Steps to Recognizing Your Worth:

1. **Reflect on Your Achievements**: Take a step back and think about the wins, both big and small, that you've had in your career and personal life. These accomplishments are evidence of your worth. It's important to regularly remind yourself of your growth and successes.

2. **Collect Feedback**: Reach out to colleagues, mentors, or peers and ask for feedback on your contributions. People who work closely with you can provide insight into your strengths and help you understand your value in a wider context.

3. **Track Your Contributions**: Keep a record of your work and successes. If you're in a role where you contribute to projects, sales numbers, or client success, have those numbers and results ready to support your claims when advocating for yourself in a raise or promotion conversation.

Building Confidence and Self-Esteem

You can know your worth intellectually, but the next step is to believe it and act on it. The confidence to advocate for yourself and demand what you deserve is built through practice and mindset shifts.

Techniques for Building Confidence:

1. **Reframe Negative Thoughts**: One of the biggest challenges for many women is the internal dialogue that tells us we're not good enough, capable enough, or deserving enough. These thoughts feed self-doubt and can lead to imposter syndrome. The truth is, those thoughts are lies. Replace them with empowering affirmations like: "I am qualified," "I am capable," "I bring value," and "I am worthy of success."

2. **Practice Self-Care**: Confidence is built not just through thoughts but through actions. Taking care of your physical and emotional well-being is crucial. When you invest in your health and well-being, you not only feel better physically but also strengthen your mental resilience. This helps you stay grounded and confident in the face of challenges.

3. **Celebrate Your Wins**: Whether it's a big victory or a small achievement, take time to celebrate your progress. Recognizing your successes reinforces the belief that you are capable and deserving of more.

    Example: The entrepreneur previously discussed who was juggling numerous partnerships also knew the importance of self-celebration. Every time she secured a new partnership or overcame a business obstacle; she took a moment to reflect on the progress she was making. This helped her maintain her confidence and stay focused on her bigger goals.

4. **Take Your Seat at the Table**: One of the most powerful ways to build confidence is to lean in. When opportunities arise, take them. Don't let fear or self-doubt hold you back. You have earned your place; don't shrink yourself to make others comfortable. Whether it's speaking up in a meeting or pitching an idea in a boardroom, show up as your full, unapologetic self.

Example: In the previous chapters, we saw a career professional who felt at times that she wasn't "ready" for the next big opportunity. But when she finally leaned in—when she stepped into her leadership potential, despite her doubts—she not only claimed her seat at the table but also helped lead her team to success.

Negotiating Your Value in Career and Personal Endeavors

Once you recognize your worth and build confidence, it's time to negotiate for what you deserve. Whether you're asking for a raise, seeking a promotion, or negotiating the terms of a business partnership, the ability to advocate for your value is one of the most important skills you can develop.

Key Strategies for Negotiating Your Worth:

1. **Know Your Market Value**: Do your research. Understand the market value for your role or industry and know what others with your level of experience and expertise are earning. This helps you enter negotiations with confidence and clarity.

   Example: Think of the corporate professional mentioned earlier: She leveraged the wisdom of both a coach and a mentor to strategically prepare for a raised conversation. She knew the value of her contributions, had hard data to back it up, and entered negotiations prepared to make her case with confidence.

2. **Prepare for Objections**: In any negotiation, you will likely face some form of pushback. Be prepared to handle objections by staying calm, reiterating your value, and focusing on the results you bring to the table.

3. **Be Willing to Walk Away**: The most powerful negotiators know when to walk away. If the terms are not aligned with your worth, be prepared to respectfully say no. Walking away is a sign of strength, not weakness, and often results in more favorable terms.

Conclusion

Knowing your worth is the foundation for everything else. When you recognize your value, you build the confidence to advocate for yourself, negotiate better opportunities, and claim your seat at the table. Imposter syndrome, fear, and self-doubt might try to hold you back, but when you lean in and take action, you prove to yourself, and the world, that you belong.

In personal and professional settings, don't let anyone make you feel less than or like you don't deserve to be there. Never doubt yourself. Never settle for less than you deserve. Your worth is not up for debate. It's time to step up, speak up, and let the world see the power of knowing your value.

Reflection:

"Don't settle for less than you deserve. Remember, you are not a product of your circumstances, but a result of your decisions." – Stephen Covey

Having explored the importance of self-awareness, integrity, boundaries, leveraging networks, and the power of collaboration, we now turn to an equally vital aspect of your journey: understanding and asserting your worth.

Reflection Questions:

1. How does self-awareness help you recognize and assert your value, and how do your strengths and boundaries contribute to knowing your worth?
2. How does maintaining integrity support your ability to advocate for your worth, and can you recall a situation where staying true to your values helped you assert yourself?
3. How do the boundaries you've established reinforce your sense of self-worth, and what strategies can you use to ensure these boundaries are respected?
4. How can collaboration with others help you appreciate your unique contributions and increase your confidence?
5. Reflect on a time you experienced imposter syndrome. How did it affect your decisions, and what techniques can you use to overcome self-doubt and reaffirm your worth?

Notes

CHAPTER 7

Unlock Your Growth Mindset and Uncover a World of Endless Possibilities

Throughout this book, we've focused on building a strong foundation of self-awareness, integrity, healthy boundaries, collaboration, and knowing your worth. These principles are essential for fostering both personal and professional growth. But one of the most powerful catalysts for growth is the ability to unlock and fully embrace a growth mindset.

A growth mindset is a belief that abilities and intelligence can be developed through dedication, effort, and the willingness to learn. It's about seeing challenges not as obstacles, but as opportunities to stretch and evolve. When you adopt this mindset, you open yourself up to a world of possibilities, new opportunities, fresh perspectives, and a deeper sense of resilience. This chapter will explore how to cultivate and maintain a growth mindset, as well as how to embrace challenges and failure as part of your journey toward success.

Author Tony Robbins says, "There is no growth in comfort and no comfort in growth." This quote beautifully captures the essence of a growth mindset. Growth often happens in places of discomfort, where you challenge yourself, push your limits, and step outside your comfort zone. It's in those moments of struggle that the greatest learning and growth take place.

The Concept of a Growth Mindset vs. a Fixed Mindset

Before we dive into how to unlock your growth mindset, let's first understand the difference between a growth mindset and a fixed mindset.

- **Fixed Mindset**: People with a fixed mindset believe that their abilities, intelligence, and talents are static, that they are either good at something or they aren't. They avoid challenges, fear failure, and may give up easily when faced with obstacles because they believe their abilities are limited. They often see mistakes as reflections of their inability, rather than as opportunities to learn.

- **Growth Mindset**: People with a growth mindset believe that their abilities can be developed through hard work, perseverance, and learning. They embrace challenges as opportunities for growth, seek out constructive feedback, and view failure as part of the learning process. They are more likely to persist through difficulties and, as a result, achieve greater success.

Example: Consider the career professional from earlier in the book. Early in her journey, she struggled with self-doubt, believing that her skills and abilities were limited by her education and past experiences. But as she worked with her coach and mentor, she began to shift her thinking. She started to view setbacks not as failures but as lessons, opportunities to adapt, refine her approach, and keep moving forward. With each new challenge, she learned more about herself and her potential, and her confidence grew exponentially. She was embracing the power of a growth mindset and letting it fuel her career success.

How to Cultivate and Maintain a Growth Mindset

The beauty of a growth mindset is that it can be developed and nurtured at any point in life. It requires a shift in how we view our abilities, setbacks, and successes. The key to unlocking your growth mindset is self-awareness, commitment, and resilience.

Here are several strategies for cultivating and maintaining a growth mindset:

1. **Embrace Challenges**: Start seeing challenges as opportunities rather than threats. When you encounter a difficult situation, resist the urge to shy away. Instead, ask yourself, "What can I learn from this? How can I grow?" By tackling challenges head-on, you expand your capacity for learning and growth.

   Example: In Chapter 3, the aspiring executive was confronted with the daunting challenge of stepping into a senior management role. At first, the task seemed overwhelming, and she questioned her readiness. However, by embracing the challenge with an open mind, she saw it as a chance to expand her leadership skills and grow into a more strategic role. She adopted a growth mindset, accepted the challenge, and found new levels of capability within herself.

2. **View Failure as a Learning Opportunity**: Instead of seeing failure as a reflection of your inadequacies, reframe it as a learning opportunity. Failure is an inevitable part of the growth process. Every failure provides insight into what doesn't work and what can be improved next time.

   Example: The entrepreneur we've been following faced a significant setback when her business venture didn't take off as expected. Rather than giving up, she treated this failure as valuable feedback—an opportunity to refine her strategy and approach. She asked herself, "What went wrong? What can I learn from this?" By using failure as a tool for growth, she was able to pivot and ultimately create a thriving business.

3. **Seek Feedback and Act on It**: People with a growth mindset actively seek feedback from others. They understand that feedback, whether positive or constructive, is invaluable for their development. Be open to feedback from coaches, mentors, colleagues, or even clients. Use that feedback to make improvements and adjust your approach.

   Example: Remember the corporate professional from Chapter 3 who had been seeking mentorship and coaching. She regularly asked for feedback from her mentor and peers, not just to gauge how she was doing but to improve and grow. This openness to feedback allowed her to refine her skills and approach, which helped her stand out as a rising leader in her organization.

4. **Focus on Effort, Not Just Results**: People with a growth mindset understand that the journey is just as important as the destination. Instead of focusing solely on the outcome, focus on the effort you put into the process. Hard work and dedication are key elements in growth, regardless of the result.

5. **Challenge Negative Self-Talk**: When faced with self-doubt or imposter syndrome, challenge the

negative thoughts that arise. Remind yourself of your strengths, your progress, and the skills you've developed over time. The more you reframe negative thoughts, the easier it becomes to stay focused on growth.

Opening Yourself Up to Endless Possibilities for Growth and Success

When you operate with a growth mindset, you open yourself up to a world of endless possibilities. You stop limiting yourself with preconceived notions of what you can or can't do. With a growth mindset, you begin to see that there is no ceiling to what you can achieve. This is where opportunity and innovation thrive.

1. **Open Yourself to New Learning**: Whether it's through books, courses, mentorship, or new experiences, always be open to learning. Growth doesn't happen in isolation—it happens when you continually seek new knowledge, perspectives, and challenges.

2. **Take Risks and Step Out of Your Comfort Zone**: Growth happens when you're willing to take risks and step into the unknown. Yes, it's uncomfortable. But that discomfort is a signal that you're growing. Take small risks that push your boundaries and gradually expand your comfort zone.

3. **Look for New Opportunities**: A growth mindset allows you to recognize new opportunities that might have once seemed out of reach. Whether it's a new career path, a new project, or a personal venture, you'll see these as possibilities rather than obstacles.

   Example: The **entrepreneur** who initially faced failure in her first business venture embraced her growth mindset and leveraged her network, skills, and new learning to spot opportunities that others missed. She took calculated risks, launched a new business, and achieved success beyond her expectations.

Conclusion

Unlocking your growth mindset is one of the most transformative things you can do for yourself. It shifts how you view the world and your place within it. A growth mindset empowers you to take on challenges, view failure as a learning opportunity, and embrace the idea that you can always improve, always evolve, and always grow.

When you cultivate and sustain this mindset, you step into a world of endless possibilities. No longer constrained by a fixed idea of what's possible, you embrace each day as an opportunity to learn, grow, and achieve things you once thought were out of reach.

As you continue on your journey, remember: Growth is a process, not a destination. Embrace it. Own it. And most importantly, never stop believing in your ability to unlock your potential and create the life and career you truly desire.

Remember to embrace the discomfort, lean into the process, and watch yourself flourish.

Reflection:

"I never lose. I either win or learn." – *Nelson Mandela*

With a growth mindset in place, you've opened yourself to a world of possibilities and embraced the journey of continuous improvement. Now, let's explore how to harness this mindset to innovate and lead with impact in both your personal and professional life.

Reflection Questions:

1. How has developing self-awareness helped you apply a growth mindset, and how has this enhanced your personal or professional life?
2. How does maintaining integrity support your growth mindset, and can you share an instance where it helped you navigate a challenge?
3. How do healthy boundaries contribute to sustaining a growth mindset, and how can they help you focus on growth opportunities without feeling overwhelmed?
4. How can collaborating with others who have a growth mindset amplify your own growth, and can you describe a time when this mutual growth occurred?
5. How does recognizing your worth empower you to take risks and embrace challenges, and how can this fuel your commitment to continuous learning and development?

Notes

CHAPTER 8

Conclusion

As we reach the end of this journey, let's reflect on the principles we've explored and the powerful impact they can have on your personal and professional life. These principles are not just theoretical—they are actionable strategies, tested and proven to transform how you approach challenges, set goals, and make decisions. They serve as the foundation for your growth, guiding you toward realizing your fullest potential.

Here's a summary of the key principles that can lead to extraordinary results:

1. **Understand Who You Are and What You Want**
   Self-awareness is the cornerstone of all growth. Knowing who you are, what drives you, and what truly matters to you sets the stage for everything else. Once you are clear on your values and purpose, you can make decisions that are aligned with your true

self—decisions that propel you toward your goals, not away from them.

2. **Never Compromise Your Morals or Values**
Integrity is non-negotiable. Your values are your compass, guiding you through tough decisions and difficult circumstances. When you stay true to what you believe in, no matter what, you build trust in yourself and in those around you. This unwavering commitment to your values becomes a powerful force in your career and personal life.

3. **Leverage Your Network and Exhaust All Resources**
No one achieves success alone. The right people—mentors, coaches, peers, sponsors, and advocates—are your greatest assets. By cultivating and nurturing meaningful relationships and leveraging all available resources, you open yourself to knowledge, opportunities, and support that can accelerate your growth. Your network is not just a collection of names; it's a dynamic resource to propel you forward.

4. **Operate Within Your Boundaries**
Setting and maintaining boundaries is essential for sustaining your energy, focus, and long-term success. Boundaries help you protect your time, preserve your well-being, and ensure that your actions remain aligned with your values. When you honor these boundaries—both with yourself and others—you

avoid burnout and keep your life balanced and purpose-driven.

5. **Collaborate, Don't Compete**
   True success isn't a zero-sum game. Secure individuals collaborate, leveraging the strengths of others to create collective success. By moving away from a competitive mindset and toward a collaborative one, you unlock new opportunities for growth and innovation. Together, we can achieve far more than we ever could alone.

6. **Know Your Worth**
   Recognizing and advocating for your worth is one of the most empowering actions you can take. Confidence doesn't come from waiting for others to affirm you—it comes from knowing what you bring to the table. When you know your value, you can advocate for it in both personal and professional situations, ensuring that you receive the opportunities, compensation, and respect you deserve.

7. **Unlock Your Growth Mindset and Uncover a World of Endless Possibilities**
   Embrace the idea that growth is limitless. A growth mindset opens doors to new learning, new experiences, and new possibilities. It shifts your perspective from fear of failure to a desire for continuous improvement. By adopting this mindset, you embrace

challenges, overcome setbacks, and keep expanding your potential—knowing that you are capable of achieving things you never thought possible.

Encouragement to Take Action

These principles are not just to be read—they are to be implemented. It's easy to get caught up in the theory, but it's in action that transformation happens. Every day, you have the power to make choices that align with your values, stretch your boundaries, and take you one step closer to the life you want to live.

The strategies discussed in this book are designed to help you unlock your potential. Start by choosing one principle to focus on. Make it a habit. Then layer in the others. Start small but commit to consistent progress. The process will be challenging, but I assure you—it will be worth it. The journey toward unlocking your full potential is about showing up for yourself every single day, no matter the circumstances.

Final Words of Inspiration

Now is your time. The world is waiting for you to claim your seat at the table. You are capable, you are worthy, and you are MORE THAN enough.

Regardless of where you are on your journey, whether you're just beginning or have already achieved remarkable milestones, there is always room to grow. The power to unlock your potential lives within you, but it requires commitment, resilience, and the courage to show up for yourself every single day.

Growth is a continuous journey, not a destination. The road ahead may test you, but it is through those very challenges that you rise, transform, and step into your full power. Every obstacle is an invitation to evolve, every setback is a setup for a comeback, and every small step forward is a triumph.

So take a deep breath, trust the process, lean on your village, and walk boldly into the life you were meant to live.

Notes

Notes

Notes

Notes

Notes

Notes

Notes

Notes

Notes

CHAPTER 8: Conclusion

Notes

Notes

CHAPTER 8: Conclusion

Notes

Notes

CHAPTER 8: Conclusion

Notes

Notes

Notes

Notes

CHAPTER 8: Conclusion

Notes

Notes

Notes

Notes

www.ingramcontent.com/pod-product-compliance
Lightning Source LLC
Chambersburg PA
CBHW071223160426
43196CB00012B/2396